FOR THOSE WHO W...
OF PEACE THAT ...

OVERCOMING FEAR AND ANXIETY WITH THE

WORD OF GOD

WESLEY LEWIS

Overcoming Fear & Anxiety with the Word of God: For Those Who Want to Discover the Promise of Peace that Surpasses Understanding. Copyright © 2021 Wesley Lewis.

All rights reserved. No part of this publication may be reproduced, distributed, or transmitted, including photocopying, recording,
or other electronic or mechanical methods, without the prior written permission of the publisher, except in the case of brief quotations embodied in critical reviews and certain other noncommercial uses permitted by copyright law. To request permission, write to the author via the website below:

www.wesleyrejoiced.com

Quoted Scripture is from the ESV® Bible (The Holy Bible, English Standard Version®) copyright © 2001 by Crossway Bibles, a publishing ministry of Good News Publishers. ESV Text Edition: 2016. The ESV® text has been reproduced in cooperation with and by permission of Good News Publishers. Unauthorized reproduction of this publication is prohibited. All rights reserved.

The ESV® Bible (The Holy Bible, English Standard Version®) is adapted from the Revised Standard Version of the Bible, copyright Division of Christian Education of the National Council of the Churches of Christ in the U.S.A. All rights reserved.

ISBN: 978-0-578-98976-1

Contents

Introduction .... - 1 -

Preface .... - 3 -

Part 1 – The Power of Thought .... - 5 -

Part 2 –Triumph Over .... - 12 -

the Spirit of Fear .... - 12 -

Part 3 – Fighting Fear with Scripture .... - 28 -

Part 4 – Renouncing and Declaring .... - 52 -

Part 5 – Praying Scripture Out Loud .... - 60 -

Concluding Prayer .... - 71 -

Review and Activation .... - 73 -

A Note from the Author .... - 77 -

Dedication

This book is dedicated to the children and youth of Faitihchild Ministries.

You forever have my heart. Although so many of you have grown up my prayers will go with you all the days of my life. To the ones that started it all, the ones who I now see every week, the ones that I have yet to meet, and the ones that are not yet born– may this book be a testimony to you of what you have heard and will surely hear me proclaim to you year after year:

The Lord is near, the Lord is faithful, the Lord is bigger than any storm you will ever face. Cry out to him and he will answer you. You are sons and daughters of the Most High God and you are chosen for such a time as this. Rise up and bring Jesus his full reward.

With Love and Thanksgiving,

Miss Wesley

Introduction

 My entire childhood I was tormented by fear. It was the enemy's primary weapon against me. I didn't know what I was fighting against and so I did not know how to fight. My journey battling fear and anxiety took me to a place of severe depression at a very young age. It wasn't until I was in my Junior year of High School that I began the journey to freedom with Jesus.

I have gained freedom from fear by the power of Christ and my heart longs to see others who suffer the way I did set free.

It is our birthright in Christ to be free of the grasp of the enemy, fear included. I have prayerfully written this book as a tool for the people of God to use when battling fear and anxiety. It is a book that would have changed my life when I was a little girl. It is my prayer that it blesses all who read it and that the church will be further equipped, not only to be free themselves, but to set the captives free who long to know the Prince of Peace too.

May God encounter you as you read. His words never return void and I know that the Lord will meet you within the scriptures throughout this book.

Preface

There is no other creature in Heaven or on Earth that can say what the human being can. "I am made in the image of God." All living things move and have their being because of Jesus (Acts 17:28). The angels in Heaven, the horses, the rodents, the fish that are hidden in the depths of the ocean, the grasshopper, and the scorpion only exist because God has given them life. Yet none are created in the likeness of God almighty apart from man and woman.

God Himself is three in one – Father, Son, and Holy Spirit. As we are made in his image, we also are three in one – **Body, Soul, and Spirit.**

> *"Now may the God of peace himself sanctify you completely and may your whole spirit and soul and body be kept blameless at the coming of our Lord Jesus Christ."*
> **1 Thessalonians 5:23 ESV**

We will be focusing on a specific aspect of humanity in this book: **The soul.**

Our soul reflects the heart and the mind. The mind goes beyond that of an organ. Certainly, the brain is an organ. An intricate and fascinating organ that runs our entire body. But human will, emotions, hope, fear, joy and ultimately, our THOUGHTS are connected to our souls.

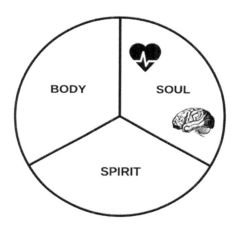

Part 1 – The Power of Thought

Our thoughts have more power than we often realize. For example, a mother may make a mistake one day. Perhaps she loses her patience and yells at her children. Or perhaps she becomes distracted and one of her children climbs up onto tall furniture and falls and injures themselves. She may have the thought, *"I am a terrible mother."*

If she believes that thought, it will produce fruit. It will create anxiety and shame within her. She may lay awake at night worrying about all the times she has made mistakes. She may worry about other issues her children are having and how she does not know how to best parent them. She then wakes up tired and stressed. So that morning she is short with her children when they fuss about getting up for school. The morning is chaotic, the children are defiant, the baby is crying, and again, she believes she is a terrible mother.

By the time her husband gets home, she is in tears, and dinner isn't prepared. He makes a comment about how the house is a mess, and this pushes her over the edge. They get into an argument, and the evening further descends into difficulty.

They don't get the children into bed until 10:30, and by the time she finally lays down, she thinks to herself again, *"I am a terrible mother."* The cycle repeats itself the next day because she still believes this thought. To break free of the cycle she needs to stop believing the lie. She needs to change her thoughts.

Sometimes these thoughts are our own. We all have moments of doubt, of fear, of stress – we ask the *"what if?"* questions.

- What if I can't pay the mortgage this month?
- What if my child gets hurt at school?
- What if I can't find a job?
- What if my parents don't come home from their trip safely?
- What if I fail this class?
- What if my family gets sick?

The list could go on forever. From small children, to teens, to adults, everyone has their own *"what if"* questions. If it were just our own minds with no influence, it would be enough. However, we are also constantly influenced by outside sources. What other people say to us, and what society says to us goes into our minds.

<u>*The most harmful voice can often be the voice of the enemy.*</u>

Satan knows that our thoughts hold this power to produce life-altering change. So his primary tactic is to attack the mind. If we are in Christ Jesus, we know that Christ has overcome all things and that Satan is defeated. The enemy knows this as well – but he also knows how to lie about it. He will continue to lie to us until we reach paradise. It is all he has left against the people of God. He knows if we believe a lie, he can gain a stronghold – something in our lives that he clings to in order to attack us.

> *"He was a murderer from the beginning, and does not stand in the truth, because there is no truth in him. When he lies, he speaks out of his own character, for he is a liar and the father of lies."* **John 8:44 ESV**

Our war with fear and anxiety resides within the mind first and then within the heart. It reaches the heart if it can penetrate the mind. It is our responsibility to decide what thoughts to entertain.

CALL TO ACTION

1. Reject the thoughts that do not align with the Word of God.

To reject them means to…

    a. Recognize that it's not of God
    b. Refuse to entertain the thought
    c. Partner with thoughts that align with the truth of God's Word

"For the weapons of our warfare are not of the flesh but have divine power to destroy strongholds. We destroy arguments and every lofty opinion raised against the knowledge of God, and take every thought captive to obey Christ,"
2 Corinthians 10:4-5 ESV

"Set your minds on things that are above, not on things that are on earth."
Colossians 3:2 ESV

"And he said to him, 'You shall love the Lord your God with all your heart and with all your soul and with all your mind.'"
Matthew 22:37 ESV

"Finally, brothers, whatever is true, whatever is honorable, whatever is just, whatever is pure, whatever is lovely, whatever is commendable, if

there is any excellence, if there is anything worthy of praise, think about these things."
Philippians 4:8 ESV

"Do not be conformed to this world, but be transformed by the renewal of your mind, that by testing you may discern what is the will of God, what is good and acceptable and perfect."
Romans 12:2 ESV

"Be sober-minded; be watchful. Your adversary the devil prowls around like a roaring lion, seeking someone to devour."
1 Peter 5:8 ESV

"Therefore, preparing your minds for action, and being sober-minded, set your hope fully on the grace that will be brought to you at the revelation of Jesus Christ."
1 Peter 1:13 ESV

"For those who live according to the flesh set their minds on the things of the flesh, but those who live according to the Spirit set their minds on the things of the Spirit. For to set the mind on the flesh is death, but to set the mind on the Spirit is life and peace."

Romans 8:5-6 ESV

"Keep your heart with all vigilance, for from it flow the springs of life."
Proverbs 4:23 ESV

Guarding the heart and the mind is a daily journey. The only way to defend ourselves from that which is not of God is to know that which is <u>OF God</u>. To do this, we need to...

CALL TO ACTION

② Know the Word of God

Instead of asking the question, "What if I fail?" or, "What if something bad happens?" we need to ask the question, "What does God say about this?"

IN SUMMARY - THE POWER OF THOUGHT

- The human is Body, Soul, and Spirit (1 Thessalonians 5:23)
- The soul represents the mind and the heart
- Thoughts enter the mind and impact the heart when they are entertained
- Satan/the demonic realm attacks the mind and hopes that the person will entertain thoughts that stand in opposition to truth
- Thoughts that are entertained impact our soul and turn into our reality

TAKE ACTION

- Recognize the source of the thought
    - Your own thought
    - God
    - The Enemy

- Refuse to accept and entertain any thought that stands in opposition to the Word of God

- Focus your mind on the Word of God and align your thoughts with the thoughts of God

Part 2 – Triumph Over the Spirit of Fear

We are in Christ, and so this is the truth, "For God gave us a spirit not of fear but of POWER and LOVE and SELF-CONTROL."

2 Timothy 1:7 ESV

Fear is indeed a spirit. This is not to say that every time we feel afraid it is demonically influenced. However, there are many times that the spirit of fear does play a part. The spirit of fear insights us to worry, to lay awake at night, to ask those *"what if"* questions that torment so many minds. This spirit crouches at the door waiting for any opportunity.

"Be sober-minded; be watchful. Your adversary the devil prowls around like a roaring lion, seeking someone to devour."

1 Peter 5:8 ESV

It attacks parents with thoughts of sick and dying children. It attacks children with thoughts of parents that don't return home. It often comes suddenly at calculated moments.

A person is driving in their car, and suddenly, they have a thought of being in a terrible accident. A doctor is eating his lunch in the hospital cafeteria, and images of flatlining patients flood his mind. A child is lying in bed, and the thought of something lurking in the darkness makes him burst into tears. He cries out for his mother with no explanation. A girl sits in her Sunday School classroom, and her heart begins to race as she thinks, "what if I don't make it to Heaven?"

CALL TO ACTION

 ## DON'T Give Fear an Open Door

Everyone that has lived has experienced some level of these sudden thoughts and feelings, fiery arrows that insight panic. Some come with no other explanation than Satan hates us and wants us to live in fear. Yet we are also responsible for guarding our heart and our mind.

Remember that the enemy seeks a foothold. The spirit of fear and anxiety will cling to anything that you give to it.

> "...and give no opportunity to the devil."
> **Ephesians 4:27 ESV**

I often hear the youth that I minister to tell me of how they are afraid due to a horror movie that they watched or some terrible thing they saw online. I remember years ago when I started watching a movie on Netflix about a serial killer. There was a terrible scene in the beginning that I hadn't expected, and I was hit with such a fierce spirit of fear. I flipped the television off immediately and *renounced* it out loud.

I invited the Holy Spirit and focused on the truth of God's Word. I knew there was a demonic attachment to the movie. As suspected, when I looked up the story behind it, I found it was based on the true story of a Satanist who was convicted of multiple killings. The enemy was feeding off the retelling of the story, and it was pleased to attack when I saw the scene.

What is Renouncing?

Renounce: "formally declare one's abandonment of (a claim, right, or possession)."

- Give up
- Relinquish
- Abandon
- Resign
- Disclaim

When I say that I renounce the spirit of fear, I out loud declare that I sever all partnership and attachment with it. If I have invited it, even unknowingly, I cast it off. I reject it in its fullness.

For example, if one has partnered with a demonic lie that they are unworthy, they formerly reject it as a part of walking into freedom from it.

"I repent Lord Jesus of entertaining the lie that I am not worthy. By your blood and your sacrifice, I am worthy. You have bought me with a price. I renounce the lie that I am unworthy in Jesus' name. I receive the truth of God's word about my identity in Christ."

When we do open the door we can repent, renounce, and walk into truth. Yet, we must grow in our self-control of what we ourselves input or allow into our minds and our hearts. It is my personal conviction not to watch films or read books that glorify demonic attack, gore, and things of the occult. It is not edifying to my spirit, and what we put into our minds enters our heart.

> *"Above all else, guard your heart, it is the wellspring of life."*
> **Proverbs 4:23 ESV**

The Spirit of God Leads us Into Truth

God has not given us a spirit of fear – he has given us a spirit of <u>power</u>, <u>love</u>, and <u>self-control</u>. The Holy Spirit indwells within us. Furthermore, the Holy Spirit reminds us of the Word of God. When the spirit of fear attacks, the Spirit of God helps us to stay firmly planted on the Word of God.

> *"But the Helper, the Holy Spirit, whom the Father will send in my name, he will teach you all things and bring to your remembrance all that I have said to you."*
> **John 14:26 ESV**

Scripture is God's gift to us. It's a roadmap to everything that we do. It is also a powerful weapon against the enemy, against lies, and against temptations. Even Satan himself used scripture to tempt Jesus in the desert. When Satan uses scripture, he twists it and quotes it out of context. So, we must know what the Word actually says. When Satan tempted Jesus with scripture, Jesus responded by using scripture correctly. This displays for us that we cannot overcome without scripture. It is the Living Word of God.

> *"For the word of God is living and active, sharper than any two-edged sword, piercing to*

> *the division of soul and of spirit, of joints and of marrow, and discerning the thoughts and intentions of the heart."*
> **Hebrews 4:12 ESV**

> *"All Scripture is breathed out by God and profitable for teaching, for reproof, for correction, and for training in righteousness,"*
> **2 Timothy 3:16 ESV**

Scripture is...
- Living and active
- Sharper than any two-edged sword
- Piercing to the division of soul and spirit and body
- Discerning the heart
- Breathed out by God

Jesus says this of His Words...
> *"Everyone then who hears these words of mine and does them will be like a wise man who built his house on the rock. And the rain fell, and the floods came, and the winds blew and beat on that house, but it did not fall, because it had been founded on the rock."*
> **Matthew 7:24-25 ESV**

The Lord does not promise us that we will not face opposition. To the contrary, he warns us that we surely will. He also promises us that he will give us wisdom during it.

> *"Count it all joy, my brothers, when you meet trials of various kinds, for you know that the testing of your faith produces steadfastness. And let steadfastness have its full effect, that you may be perfect and complete, lacking in nothing. If any of you lacks wisdom, let him ask God, who gives generously to all without reproach, and it will be given him. But let him ask in faith, with no doubting, for the one who doubts is like a wave of the sea that is driven and tossed by the wind."*
>
> **James 1:2-6 ESV**

Satan doesn't want us focused on doing the work of the Lord. He doesn't want us to rest easy, to sleep in peace, to bring peace with us into the midst of chaos, to pray over others to receive peace, to find joy in the presence of God, day to day. On the contrary, Satan wants us distracted by fear and doubt. He knows that if we remain in this place that we will be far less effective at sharing Christ with others, caring for others, and worshipping God.

The Lord knows this, and He has fully equipped us to face it. **Christ has full dominion, and Christ lives within us.**

> *"And to him was given dominion and glory and a kingdom, that all peoples, nations, and languages should serve him; his dominion is an everlasting dominion, which shall not pass away, and his kingdom on that shall not be destroyed."*
> ***Daniel 7:14 ESV***

> *"Behold, I have given you authority to tread on serpents and scorpions, and over all the power of the enemy, and nothing shall hurt you."*
> ***Luke 10:19 ESV***

God is perfect love, and through Jesus, perfect love is demonstrated to us. **This perfect love casts out fear. Dwell on the love of Christ as he dwells in you.** Do not allow Satan to steal your peace when Jesus is the Prince of Peace who gives this to you as a birthright.

> *"There is no fear in love, but perfect love casts out fear. For fear has to do with punishment,*

> *and whoever fears has not been perfected in love."*
>
> **1 John 4:18 ESV**

CALL TO ACTION

Put on the Armor of God Daily

We have head knowledge of who Christ is and how he dwells within us. Yet we must put this into practice. The apostle Paul says...

> *"Finally, be strong in the Lord and in the strength of his might. Put on the whole armor of God, that you may be able to stand against the schemes of the devil. For we do not wrestle against flesh and blood, but against the rulers, against the authorities, against the cosmic powers over this present darkness, against the spiritual forces of evil in the heavenly places. Therefore, take up the whole armor of God, that you may be able to withstand in the evil day, and having done all, to stand firm. Stand therefore, having fastened on the belt of truth, and having put on the breastplate of*

> *righteousness, and, as shoes for your feet, having put on the readiness given by the gospel of peace. In all circumstances take up the shield of faith, with which you can extinguish all the flaming darts of the evil one; and take the helmet of salvation, and the sword of the Spirit, which is the word of God, praying at all times in the Spirit, with all prayer and supplication. To that end, keep alert with all perseverance, making supplication for all the saints,"*
> **Ephesians 6:10-18 ESV**

1. The Belt of Truth

> *Jesus said to him, "I am the way, and the truth, and the life. No one comes to the Father except through me."*
> **John 14:6 ESV**

The belt of the soldier's armor is necessary for the rest of the armor to be in place. In order to have any part of God's Kingdom we must have truth. It is the truth that leads us into the arms of the Father.

2. The Breastplate of Righteousness

> *"For our sake he made him to be sin who knew no sin, so that in him we might become the righteousness of God."*
> **2 Corinthians 5:21 ESV**

The breastplate of the soldier's armor guards the heart. We are made righteous/holy by the work of Jesus on the cross and the grave. He gives us a clean and new heart. Then the Holy Spirit brings us through the process of sanctification where we grow in our obedience daily.

3. The Shoes of the Gospel of Peace

> *"Peace I leave with you; my peace I give to you. Not as the world gives do I give to you. Let not your hearts be troubled, neither let them be afraid."*
> **John 14:27 ESV**

How far can a soldier travel without their shoes? We are to walk in peace and bring peace into every place that we go. The Gospel means "Good News." It is the news that Christ Jesus has come to bring salvation, joy, hope, restoration, and REST to the weary.

4. The Shield of Faith

> *"Now faith is the assurance of things hoped for,
> the conviction of things not seen."*
> **Hebrews 11:1 ESV**

The soldier's shield is held up when under enemy attack. It blocks the fiery arrows from hitting them because they cannot penetrate through iron. Our faith is to go far beyond what we can see with our natural eyes. Doubt is quickly extinguished when we hold fast to faith.

5. The Helmet of Salvation

> *"For I am sure that neither death nor life, nor angels nor rulers, nor things present nor things to come, nor powers, nor height nor depth, nor anything else in all creation, will be able to separate us from the love of God in Christ Jesus our Lord."*
> **Romans 8:38-39 ESV**

The helmet protects the soldier's brain – the mind. Satan loves to come in and accuse - insert thoughts of condemnation and allegations. He can't take our salvation, so he tries to make us question it. Jesus doesn't question our salvation and we shouldn't either.

6. The Sword of the Spirit

In His right hand He held seven stars, and out of His mouth came a sharp two-edged sword; and His face was like the sun shining in its strength."

Revelation 1:16 ESV

<u>The Word of God is your sword</u>. It is the very essence of Christ Himself. Scripture will not help you if it simply sits on your bookshelf. The Word of God needs to be written on your heart. Eat of it like food. Jesus quoted **Deuteronomy 8:3** to the Devil, saying,

"Man does not live on bread alone but on every Word that comes from the mouth of God."

Matthew 4:4 ESV

Put on the armor of God. We must remind ourselves to proactively walk in what God has given us – righteousness, peace, faith, assured in our salvation, with the Word of God imbedded onto our hearts, minds, and coming out of our mouths.

Read the Word of God daily! Listen to it, meditate on it over and over, speak it out loud when you rise and when you go to bed, write it down in your journal, post it on your refrigerator, hang it on your wall, sing it, shout it, proclaim it, declare it, repeat it to yourself all day, and never put it down. This is our gift from God to walk in truth. It is by these words that we were able to attain salvation. It is written,

> *"So, faith comes from hearing, and hearing through the word of Christ."*
> **Romans 10:17 ESV**

My constant focus from scripture when I had rededicated my life to Christ at age 17 was…

> *"Trust in the LORD with all your heart, and do not lean on your own understanding. In all your ways acknowledge him, and he will make straight your paths."*
> **Proverbs 3:5-6 ESV**

This scripture has carried me through extremely hard moments in life, and there are thousands more scriptures to stand on.

<u>Your life will change, and your fears will flee when you lean onto the Word of God instead of your own thoughts and the thoughts of the world.</u> When you hold fast to the Word of God, the spirit of fear cannot remain, it cannot win, it cannot overcome, and you will walk into freedom.

> *"So, Jesus said to the Jews who had believed him, 'If you abide in my word, you are truly my disciples, and you will know the truth, and the truth will set you free."*
> ***John 8:31-32 ESV***

IN SUMMARY - TRIUMPH OVER THE SPIRIT OF FEAR

- Don't invite images, words, and communications into your mind and heart that give a foothold to the enemy

- Renounce, reject, and relinquish any partnership you have had with these things

- Read the Word of God so you know what truth is

- Invite the Holy Spirit to remind you of His Words

- Put on the whole Armor of God daily! (Eph 6:10-18)

    - The Belt of Truth
    - The Breastplate of Righteousness
    - The Shoes of the Gospel of Peace
    - The Shield of Faith
    - The Helmet of Salvation
    - The Sword of the Spirit

Part 3 – Fighting Fear with Scripture

When I was a little girl, my family went up into the California mountains to a Christian family camp every summer for a week. One summer, when I was about nine years old, I remember that I was suffering from terrible anxiety. I was the oldest of three children, and our family of five was staying in a small cabin. At bedtime one night I was overcome with tormenting fear of the future. My little mind was flooded with *"what if"* questions. They had come suddenly in the evening, conveniently inciting a panic attack just as my mother had gotten the baby to sleep in the little portable crib.

It went on for a very long time while I cried, and my parents, God bless them, simply did not understand why I would go into these sudden bouts of despair and fear. They were becoming agitated, which further added to my anxiety. My father must have received revelation from the Holy Spirit that night because he seemed to understand that it was a spiritual attack. Our church never spoke of such things, and I had no concept of spiritual warfare, nor did my parents. I remember that he handed me the Bible and told me to read it in the little bathroom of the cabin because the rest of the cabin was dark, and they wanted my brothers to go to sleep.

I stood there between the sink and the toilet sobbing, and I opened the huge book. It was such a large book for a child, and I didn't know where to start. The first passage I came across was Cain killing his brother, Abel. This simply made me more troubled in spirit, and I cried harder in frustration of not knowing how to comfort myself with the scriptures. I do not remember how I got to sleep that night, but I suppose at some point I wore myself out and crawled into my bunk out of sheer exhaustion.

I remember that despair of not knowing where to find the words that I was looking for; words to comfort my fearful heart. It is my desire, and God's, that those who are fearful would know what the Lord says. The body of Christ needs to be equipped for themselves and for their children. For this reason, I have compiled scriptures to use in battle against common fears.

As you read them, invite the Holy Spirit to reveal truth to you and help you to understand. Take the ones that you need most and put them up in your home where you can see them.

Memorize them so that you can think of them in moments of
out loud and tell him to flee in Jesus' name.

Fear of Failure

*"Come to me, all who labor and are heavy laden, and I will give
you rest. Take my yoke upon you, and learn from me, for I am
gentle and lowly in heart, and you will find rest for your souls.
For my yoke is easy, and my burden is light."*
Matthew 11:28-30 ESV

*"My flesh and my heart may fail, but God is the strength of my
heart and my portion forever."*
Psalm 73:26 ESV

*"For the righteous falls seven times and rises again, but the
wicked stumble in times of calamity."*
Proverbs 24:16 ESV

*"Cast your burden on the LORD, and he will sustain you; he will
never permit the righteous to be moved."*
Psalm 55:22 ESV

*"But God shows his love for us in that while we were still sinners,
Christ died for us."*
Romans 5:8 ESV

"And we know that for those who love God all things work together for good, for those who are called according to his purpose."
Romans 8:28 ESV

"The steps of a man are established by the LORD, when he delights in his way; though he fall, he shall not be cast headlong, for the LORD upholds his hand."
Psalm 37:23-24 ESV

"Rejoice not over me, O my enemy when I fall, I shall rise; when I sit in darkness, the LORD will be a light to me."
Micah 7:8 ESV

Fear of Abandonment

"For my father and my mother have forsaken me, but the LORD will take me in."
Psalm 27:10 ESV

"Can a woman forget her nursing child, that she should have no compassion on the son of her womb? Even these may forget, yet I will not forget you. Behold, I have engraved you on the palms of my hands; your walls are continually before me."
Isaiah 49:15-16 ESV

"Look to the right and see: there is none who takes notice of me; no refuge remains to me; no one cares for my soul. I cry to you, O LORD; I say, 'You are my refuge, my portion in the land of the living.'"
Psalm 142:4-5 ESV

"For the LORD loves justice; he will not forsake his saints. They are preserved forever, but the children of the wicked shall be cut off."
Psalm 37:28 ESV

"God settles the solitary in a home; he leads out the prisoners to prosperity, but the rebellious dwell in a parched land."
Psalm 68:6 ESV

"Cast me not away from your presence, and take not your Holy Spirit from me."
Psalm 51:11 ESV

"Father of the fatherless and protector of widows is God in his holy habitation."
Psalm 68:5 ESV

"I will not leave you as orphans; I will come to you."

John 14:18 ESV

"No longer do I call you servants, for the servant does not know what his master is doing; but I have called you friends, for all that I have heard from my Father I have made known to you."
John 15:15 ESV

"Teaching them to observe all that I have commanded you. And behold, I am with you always, to the end of the age."
Matthew 28:20 ESV

"I have set the LORD always before me; because he is at my right hand, I shall not be shaken."
Psalm 16:8 ESV

Fear of Rejection

"For you did not receive the spirit of slavery to fall back into fear, but you have received the Spirit of adoption as sons, by whom we cry, "Abba! Father!""
Romans 8:15 ESV

"For am I now seeking the approval of man, or of God? Or am I trying to please man? If I were still trying to please man, I would not be a servant of Christ."

Galatians 1:10 ESV

"It is better to take refuge in the LORD than to trust in man."
Psalm 118:8 ESV

"For you formed my inward parts; you knitted me together in my mother's womb. I praise you, for I am fearfully and wonderfully made. Wonderful are your works; my soul knows it very well."
Psalm 139:13-14 ESV

Fear About Finances

"Therefore, I tell you, do not be anxious about your life, what you will eat or what you will drink, nor about your body, what you will put on. Is not life more than food, and the body more than clothing? Look at the birds of the air: they neither sow nor reap nor gather into barns, and yet your heavenly Father feeds them. Are you not of more value than they? And which of you by being anxious can add a single hour to his span of life? And why are you anxious about clothing? Consider the lilies of the field, how they grow: they neither toil nor spin, yet I tell you, even Solomon in all his glory was not arrayed like one of these."
Matthew 6:25-29 ESV

"Bring the full tithe into the storehouse, that there may be food in my house. And thereby put me to the test, says the LORD of hosts, if I will not open the windows of heaven for you and pour down for you a blessing until there is no more need."
Malachi 3:10 ESV

"No one can serve two masters, for either he will hate the one and love the other, or he will be devoted to the one and despise the other. You cannot serve God and money."
Matthew 6:24 ESV

"For the love of money is a root of all kinds of evils. It is through this craving that some have wandered away from the faith and pierced themselves with many pangs."
1 Timothy 6:10 ESV

"As for the rich in this present age, charge them not to be haughty, nor to set their hopes on the uncertainty of riches, but on God, who richly provides us with everything to enjoy. 18 They are to do good, to be rich in good works, to be generous and ready to share, 19 thus storing up treasure for themselves as a good foundation for the future, so that they may take hold of that which is truly life."
1 Timothy 6:17-19 ESV

"Sell your possessions and give to the needy. Provide yourselves with moneybags that do not grow old, with a treasure in the heavens that does not fail, where no thief approaches and no moth destroys."
Luke 12:33 ESV

"But seek first the kingdom of God and his righteousness, and all these things will be added to you."
Matthew 6:33 ESV

Fear of the Unknown/Future

"I sought the LORD, and he answered me and delivered me from all my fears."
Psalm 34:4 ESV

"For as the heavens are higher than the earth, so are my ways higher than your ways and my thoughts than your thoughts."
Isaiah 55:9 ESV

"And he said to his disciples, 'Therefore I tell you, do not be anxious about your life, what you will eat, nor about your body, what you will put on. For life is more than food, and the body more than clothing. Consider the ravens: they neither sow nor

reap, they have neither storehouse nor barn, and yet God feeds them. Of how much more value are you than the birds!'"
Luke 12:22-24 ESV

"For I know the plans I have for you, declares the LORD, plans for welfare and not for evil, to give you a future and a hope."
Jeremiah 29:11 ESV

"What then shall we say to these things? If God is for us, who can be against us? He who did not spare his own Son but gave him up for us all, how will he not also with him graciously give us all things? Who shall bring any charge against God's elect? It is God who justifies. Who is to condemn? Christ Jesus is the one who died – more than that, who was raised – who is at the right hand of God, who indeed is interceding for us. Who shall separate us from the love of Christ? Shall tribulation, or distress, or persecution, or famine, or nakedness, or danger, or sword?"
Romans 8:31-35 ESV

"Even though I walk through the valley of the shadow of death, I will fear no evil, for you are with me; your rod and your staff, they comfort me."
Psalm 23:4 ESV

"Do not be anxious about anything, but in everything by prayer and supplication with thanksgiving let your requests be made known to God. And the peace of God, which surpasses all understanding, will guard your hearts and your minds in Christ Jesus."
Philippians 4:6-7 ESV

"For 'everyone who calls on the name of the Lord will be saved.'"
Romans 10:13 ESV

"Therefore, do not be anxious about tomorrow, for tomorrow will be anxious for itself. Sufficient for the day is its own trouble."
Matthew 6:34 ESV

Fear of Disaster

"Keep me safe, my God, for in you I take refuge."
Psalm 16:1 ESV

Peace I leave with you; my peace I give to you. Not as the world gives do I give to you. Let not your hearts be troubled, neither let them be afraid."
John 14:27 ESV

"The LORD will keep you from all evil; he will keep your life. The LORD will keep your going out and your coming in from this time forth and forevermore."
Psalm 121:7-8 ESV

"But the Lord is faithful. He will establish you and guard you against the evil one."
2 Thessalonians 3:3 ESV

"God is our refuge and strength, a very present help in trouble."
Psalm 46:1 ESV

"The angel of the LORD encamps around those who fear him, and delivers them."
Psalm 34:7 ESV

"Though I walk in the midst of trouble, you preserve my life; you stretch out your hand against the wrath of my enemies, and your right hand delivers me."
Psalm 138:7 ESV

Fear of Enemies

"The LORD is on my side; I will not fear. What can man do to me?"

Psalm 118:6 ESV

"Be still before the LORD and wait patiently for him; fret not yourself over the one who prospers in his way, over the man who carries out evil devices!"
Psalm 37:7 ESV

"You are a hiding place for me; you preserve me from trouble; you surround me with shouts of deliverance."
Psalm 32:7 ESV

"God is our refuge and strength, a very present help in trouble."
Psalm 46:1 ESV

"Be strong and courageous. Do not fear or be in dread of them, for it is the Lord your God who goes with you. He will not leave you or forsake you."
Deuteronomy 31:6 ESV

"No weapon that is fashioned against you shall succeed, and you shall refute every tongue that rises against you in judgment. This is the heritage of the servants of the Lord and their vindication from me, declares the Lord."
Isaiah 54:17 ESV

"When I am afraid, I put my trust in you. In God, whose word I praise, in God I trust; I shall not be afraid. What can flesh do to me?"
Psalm 56:3-4 ESV

"My God, my rock, in whom I take refuge, my shield, and the horn of my salvation, my stronghold and my refuge, my savior; you save me from violence. I call upon the LORD, who is worthy to be praised, and I am saved from my enemies."
2 Samuel 22:3-4 ESV

"Beloved, never avenge yourselves, but leave it to the wrath of God, for it is written, 'Vengeance is mine, I will repay, says the Lord.'"
Romans 12:19 ESV

"The LORD will fight for you, and you have only to be silent."
Exodus 14:14 ESV

Fear of Loss of Salvation

"There is no fear in love, but perfect love casts out fear. For fear has to do with punishment, and whoever fears has not been perfected in love."
1 John 4:18 ESV

"For I am sure that neither death nor life, nor angels nor rulers, nor things present nor things to come, nor powers, nor height nor depth, nor anything else in all creation, will be able to separate us from the love of God in Christ Jesus our Lord."
Romans 8:38-39 ESV

"My sheep hear my voice, and I know them, and they follow me. I give them eternal life, and they will never perish, and no one will snatch them out of my hand."
John 10:27-28 ESV

"And they said, 'Believe in the Lord Jesus, and you will be saved, you and your household.'"
Acts 16:31 ESV

"And it shall come to pass that everyone who calls upon the name of the Lord shall be saved."
Acts 2:21 ESV

"Though you have not seen him, you love him. Though you do not now see him, you believe in him and rejoice with joy that is inexpressible and filled with glory, obtaining the outcome of your faith, the salvation of your souls."
1 Peter 1:8-9 ESV

"For by grace you have been saved through faith. And this is not your own doing; it is the gift of God, not a result of works, so that no one may boast."
Ephesians 2:8-9 ESV

"On God rests my salvation and my glory; my mighty rock, my refuge is God."
Psalm 62:7 ESV

"For the Lord himself will descend from heaven with a cry of command, with the voice of an archangel, and with the sound of the trumpet of God. And the dead in Christ will rise first. Then we who are alive, who are left, will be caught up together with them in the clouds to meet the Lord in the air, and so we will always be with the Lord."
1 Thessalonians 4:16-17 ESV

"I am the door. If anyone enters by me, he will be saved and will go in and out and find pasture."
John 10:9 ESV

"As far as the east is from the west, so far does he remove our transgressions from us."
Psalm 103:12 ESV

"But now thus says the LORD, he who created you, O Jacob, he who formed you, O Israel: 'Fear not, for I have redeemed you; I have called you by name, you are mine.'"
Isaiah 43:1 ESV

Fear for Loved Ones

"And I looked and arose and said to the nobles and to the officials and to the rest of the people, 'Do not be afraid of them. Remember the Lord, who is great and awesome, and fight for your brothers, your sons, your daughters, your wives, and your homes.'"
Nehemiah 4:14 ESV

"Casting all your anxieties on him, because he cares for you."
1 Peter 5:7 ESV

"But the steadfast love of the LORD is from everlasting to everlasting on those who fear him, and his righteousness to children's children,"
Psalm 103:17 ESV

"But let all who take refuge in you rejoice; let them ever sing for joy, and spread your protection over them, that those who love your name may exult in you."

Psalm 5:11 ESV

"See that you do not despise one of these little ones. For I tell you that in heaven their angels always see the face of my Father who is in heaven."
Matthew 18:10 ESV

"In the fear of the LORD one has strong confidence, and his children will have a refuge."
Proverbs 14:26 ESV

"Train up a child in the way he should go; even when he is old, he will not depart from it."
Proverbs 22:6 ESV

"Every word of God proves true; he is a shield to those who take refuge in him."
Proverbs 30:5 ESV

"And we know that for those who love God all things work together for good, for those who are called according to his purpose."
Romans 8:28 ESV

Fear of Sickness

"You shall serve the Lord your God, and he will bless your bread and your water, and I will take sickness away from among you."
Exodus 23:25 ESV

"Heal the sick, raise the dead, cleanse lepers, cast out demons. You received without paying; give without pay."
Matthew 10:8 ESV

"Heal the sick in it and say to them, 'The kingdom of God has come near to you.'"
Luke 10:9 ESV

"Heal me, O Lord, and I shall be healed; save me, and I shall be saved, for you are my praise."
Jeremiah 17:14 ESV

"He heals the brokenhearted and binds up their wounds."
Psalm 147:3 ESV

"But he was pierced for our transgressions; he was crushed for our iniquities; upon him was the chastisement that brought us peace, and with his wounds we are healed."
Isaiah 53:5 ESV

"But for you who fear my name, the sun of righteousness shall rise with healing in its wings. You shall go out leaping like calves from the stall."
Malachi 4:2 ESV

"Turn back, and say to Hezekiah the leader of my people, thus says the Lord, the God of David your father: I have heard your prayer; I have seen your tears. Behold, I will heal you. On the third day you shall go up to the house of the Lord."
2 Kings 20:5 ESV

"The Spirit of the Lord is upon me, because he has anointed me to proclaim good news to the poor. He has sent me to proclaim liberty to the captives and recovering of sight to the blind, to set at liberty those who are oppressed."
Luke 4:18 ESV

"But Jesus looked at them and said, 'With man this is impossible, but with God all things are possible.'"
Matthew 19:26 ESV

"For I will restore health to you, and your wounds I will heal, declares the LORD, because they have called you an outcast: 'It is Zion, for whom no one cares!'"

Jeremiah 30:17 ESV

"'Blessed are you when people hate you and when they exclude you and revile you and spurn your name as evil, on account of the Son of Man! Rejoice in that day, and leap for joy, for behold, your reward is great in heaven; for so their fathers did to the prophets.'"
 Luke 6:22-23 ESV

"If the world hates you, know that it has hated me before it hated you. If you were of the world, the world would love you as its own; but because you are not of the world, but I chose you out of the world, therefore the world hates you. Remember the word that I said to you: 'A servant is not greater than his master.' If they persecuted me, they will also persecute you. If they kept my word, they will also keep yours. But all these things they will do to you on account of my name, because they do not know him who sent me."
John 15:18-21 ESV

Fear of Death

"For I consider that the sufferings of this present time are not worth comparing with the glory that is to be revealed to us."
Romans 8:18 ESV

"And do not fear those who kill the body but cannot kill the soul. Rather fear him who can destroy both soul and body in hell."
Matthew 10:28 ESV

"Since therefore the children share in flesh and blood, he himself likewise partook of the same things, that through death he might destroy the one who has the power of death, that is, the devil, and deliver all those who through fear of death were subject to lifelong slavery."
Hebrews 2:14-15 ESV

"Then I saw a new heaven and a new earth, for the first heaven and the first earth had passed away, and the sea was no more. And I saw the holy city, new Jerusalem, coming down out of heaven from God, prepared as a bride adorned for her husband. And I heard a loud voice from the throne saying, 'Behold, the dwelling place of God is with man. He will dwell with them, and they will be his people, and God himself will be with them as their God. He will wipe away every tear from their eyes, and death shall be no more, neither shall there be mourning, nor crying, nor pain anymore, for the former things have passed away.'"
Revelation 21:1-4 ESV

"Truly, truly, I say to you, whoever hears my word and believes him who sent me has eternal life. He does not come into judgment but has passed from death to life."
John 5:24 ESV

"Jesus said to her, 'I am the resurrection and the life. Whoever believes in me, though he die, yet shall he live,'"
John 11:25 ESV

"For if we live, we live to the Lord, and if we die, we die to the Lord. So then, whether we live or whether we die, we are the Lord's."
Romans 14:8 ESV

IN SUMMARY – FIGHTING FEAR WITH SCRIPTURE

Fear of Failure
Matthew 11:28-30
Psalm 73:26
Proverbs 24:16
Psalm 55:22
Romans 5:8
Romans 8:28
Psalm 37:23-24
Micah 7:8

Fear of Abandonment
Psalm 27:10
Isaiah 49:15-16 ESV
Psalm 142:4-5 ESV
Psalm 37:28 ESV
Psalm 68:6 ESV
Psalm 51:11 ESV
Psalm 68:5 ESV
John 14:18 ESV
John 15:15 ESV
Matthew 28:20 ESV
Psalm 16:8 ESV

Fear of Rejection
Romans 8:15 ESV
Galatians 1:10 ESV
Psalm 118:8 ESV
Psalm 139:13-14 ESV

Fear of Enemies
Psalm 118:6 ESV
Psalm 37:7 ESV
Psalm 32:7 ESV
Psalm 46:1 ESV
Deuteronomy 31:6 ESV
Isaiah 54:17 ESV
Psalm 56:3-4 ESV
2 Samuel 22:3-4 ESV
Romans 12:19 ESV
Exodus 14:14 ESV

Fear About Finances
Matthew 6:25-29 ESV
Malachi 3:10 ESV
Matthew 6:24 ESV
1 Timothy 6:10 ESV
1 Timothy 6:17-19 ESV
Luke 12:33 ESV
Matthew 6:33 ESV

Fear of the Unknown/Future
Psalm 34:4 ESV
Isaiah 55:9 ESV
Luke 12:22-24 ESV
Psalm 23:4 ESV
Philippians 4:6-7 ESV
Romans 10:13 ESV
Matthew 6:34 ESV

Fear of Disaster
Psalm 16:1 ESV
John 14:27 ESV
Psalm 121:7-8 ESV
2 Thessalonians 3:3 ESV
Psalm 46:1 ESV
Psalm 34:7 ESV
Psalm 138:7 ESV

Fear of Loss of Salvation
1 John 4:18 ESV
Romans 8:38-39 ESV
John 10:27-28 ESV
Acts 16:31 ESV
Acts 2:21 ESV
1 Peter 1:8-9 ESV
Ephesians 2:8-9 ESV
Psalm 62:7 ESV
1 Thessalonians 4:16-17 ESV
John 10:9 ESV
Psalm 103:12 ESV
Isaiah 43:1 ESV

Fear for Loved Ones
Nehemiah 4:14 ESV
1 Peter 5:7 ESV
Psalm 103:17 ESV
Psalm 5:11 ESV
Matthew 18:10 ESV
Proverbs 14:26 ESV
Proverbs 22:6 ESV
Proverbs 30:5 ESV
Romans 8:28 ESV

Fear of Sickness
Exodus 23:25 ESV
Matthew 10:8 ESV
Luke 10:9 ESV
Jeremiah 17:14 ESV
Psalm 147:3 ESV
Isaiah 53:5 ESV
Malachi 4:2 ESV
2 Kings 20:5 ESV
Luke 4:18 ESV
Matthew 19:26 ESV
Jeremiah 30:17 ESV
Luke 6:22-23 ESV
John 15:18-21 ESV

Fear of Death
Romans 8:18 ESV
Matthew 10:28 ESV
Hebrews 2:14-15 ESV
Revelation 21:1-4 ESV
John 5:24 ESV
John 11:25 ESV
Romans 14:8 ESV

Part 4 – Renouncing and Declaring

*"Death and life are in the power of the tongue,
and those who love it will eat its fruits."*
Proverbs 18:21 ESV

Use your voice! Declare truth out loud. It's not about volume, but rather about authority. It's a birthright. Take the sword in your hand and use it as a child of the Living God.

When we declare truth, it shifts something in the supernatural realm. What we speak out of our mouth in faith and authority literally impacts the principalities in the heavenly realms. The declaration of the believer is meant to partner with truth, with the will of God, with the purposes of God, and with the Holy Spirit.

*"Behold, I have given you authority to tread on
serpents and scorpions, and over all the power
of the enemy, and nothing shall hurt you."*
Luke 10:19 ESV

> *"Truly, I say to you, whatever you bind on earth shall be bound in heaven, and whatever you loose on earth shall be loosed in heaven."*
> ***Matthew 18:18 ESV***

Your proclamation of truth breaks strongholds and ties that the enemy is clinging to. It severs the lies and then tramples the enemy underfoot. Furthermore, it shifts something within your own heart and mind. Do you remember God's command to the prophet Ezekiel?

> *"The hand of the L*ORD *was upon me, and he brought me out in the Spirit of the L*ORD *and set me down in the middle of the valley. It was full of bones. And he led me around among them, and behold, there were very many on the surface of the valley, and behold, they were very dry. And he said to me, "Son of man, can these bones live?" And I answered, "O Lord G*OD*, you know." Then he said to me,* ***"Prophesy over these bones, and say to them, O dry bones, hear the word of the Lord.*** *Thus says the Lord G*OD *to these bones: Behold, I will cause breath to enter you, and you shall live. And I will lay sinews upon you, and will*

*cause flesh to come upon you, and cover you with skin, and put breath in you, and you shall live, and you shall know that I am the L*ORD*."*
Ezekiel 37:1-6 ESV

Speak life! Prophecy what the Lord has spoken! Jesus has already given you these promises. It is written,

"...For the testimony of Jesus is the spirit of prophecy."
Revelation 19:10 ESV

CALL TO ACTION

Renouncing Fear and Proclaiming Faith

Below is an example of renouncing and declaring, specifically about fear and faith. It can be used in its fullness or in portions. It is meant to be a model to you but not an end all be all of what you can use when speaking a declaration.

This is meant to be spoken out loud before God. As you speak, remember your birthright in Christ. Use your voice with authority and hold fast to the promise that God has given you – that you are more than a conqueror in Jesus Christ (Romans 8:31-39)

I renounce my partnership with fear and anxiety. Jesus, I repent of any time that I have entertained fear and anxiety in my mind and heart. I refuse to partner with fear any longer. Jesus has set me free from sin and death and all the curses that come with it. I am sealed in the blood of Christ. My name is written in the Lambs book of life. The Spirit of God dwells within me.

God has not given me a spirit of fear, but of power and love and self-control. Nothing is impossible with God. I can do all things with Christ who gives me strength. My future is full of the good promises of God. Before I was born, my days were written in his book. He formed me in my mother's womb and chose me before the foundations of the Earth. My God has good plans for me. Plans to help me and not to harm me. Plans to give me hope and a future. I partner with the truth of those good plans. I partner with my destiny in Christ Jesus.

My Father is the Most High God. He is my refuge and my strength. When I cry out to him, he answers me, and he hides me in the shadow of his wings. I will walk and not grow weary. I will run and not faint. Even though I walk through the valley of the shadow of death, I will not fear evil because Christ Jesus is with me. My Father sends angels to war on my behalf. They surround me and my loved one's day and night. Even if ten thousand fall at my side, no evil will come near my tent.

My God has dominion over all things. He has power over death and hell and all the powers under Heaven and Earth. If God is for me, then who can be against me? Oh, death, where is your sting? Even death cannot hold me. I know that there is no principality or wicked person that can separate me from the love of my God. No one can pluck me out of his hand. The spirit of fear trembles at the feet of Jesus. It pleads for mercy but finds none because it has opposed a child of the Most High God.

The Lord rebuke you Satan! Cursed is the serpent of old who crawls on his belly for shame. You struck my heal and now I have crushed your head. You have been cast down and made to eat dust for all your days. You are laid low before the nations and your beauty has been stripped from you. Shame is Lucifers portion and all who fall with him. Jesus struck you down from Heaven like lightning and all your angels with you. May you be bound in darkness and chained in calamity. Fear flees from me and back to you sevenfold and sevenfold in Jesus name.

I will cast all my anxieties onto Jesus because he cares for me. His yoke is easy, and his burden is light. When I am weary, I come to him, and he gives me rest. I will trust in the Lord with all my heart. When I do not understand, I will not worry. God, your thoughts are higher than my thoughts, and your ways are higher than my ways. Make my paths straight before me. Your word, oh Lord, is a lamp unto my path and a light unto my feet. No matter if I go to the right or the left, I will hear your voice, my God, and I will walk in your ways. You go before me with cloud and fire, and you make a way when there is no way. Surely, nothing is impossible for you.

My savior has already won the battle. He has trampled the Father of Lies beneath his feet. I will partner with the words of Christ. I will build my house on the rock of Christ, and even when the storm roars around me, I will be at peace as I dwell in the fortress of the Lord. I take every thought captive that is not of God, and I command it to bow to Christ and obey him. I speak to my mind. In Jesus' name, be submitted to the Lord. I speak to my heart. In Jesus' name, be submitted to the heart of God. I have the mind of Christ, and my will is submitted to the will of God.

My soul longs for you, Lord, in a dry and weary land where there is no water. You have heard my cry, and you answer with living water. I drink, and I will never thirst again.

This river flows from within me and fills me with overpouring joy. The Lord takes my ashes and trades them for beauty. He has given me a garment of praise instead of a spirit of despair.

I have courage like David, boldness like Daniel, faith like Abraham, perseverance like Paul, authority like Esther, restoration multiplied like Job, and victory like Gideon. My God laughs at the wicked, but the righteous he shields and vindicates. May the spirit of fear hear the roar of the Lion of Judah. May fear be trampled underfoot and disgraced. The Lord declares, "Vengeance is mine." So have your vengeance, My God, my salvation, my Strong Tower. Take vengeance for what fear has stolen in my life.

Restore to me the joy of my salvation and renew my mind and my spirit by the power of the blood of the lamb. I receive your renewal, Lord Jesus. I receive the renewal of my mind. Cleanse me with hyssop, and I will be clean. Anoint my head with oil. My cup overflows. I love your laws, Lord. I meditate on them day and night. Write them on my mind and my heart. Wherever I go, I proclaim the words of the Lord.

So now I know the truth, and the truth has set me free. Who the Son sets free is free indeed. I am free in Jesus Christ. I am free indeed. Peace is my portion today and forever. Amen.

IN SUMMARY – RENOUNCING AND DECLARING

1. The power of life and death is in the tongue (Proverbs 18:21)

2. You have God given authority to use your voice against the enemy (Luke 10:19)

3. You have God given authority to bind and loose with your voice. (Matthew 16:19)

Take Action

- Renounce: refute, cast off, reject, break agreement out loud...
    - all partnership with the spirit of fear

- Declare what God has already declared

- Declare scripture

- Declare the promises of God

- Declare death to the things of the enemy, "The Lord rebuke you Satan." (Zechariah 3:2)

- Declare life to the things of God, "Prophecy to these bones son of man that they may live." (Ezekiel 37:4)

Part 5 – Praying Scripture Out Loud

Praying scripture out loud over yourself and others in times of trouble is a powerful weapon of warfare. Years ago, I went home and visited family and was speaking to my little brother about the scriptures. He was about 13 years old at the time. I felt led to tell him about **Psalm 91** which is about divine and angelic protection. The Holy Spirit impressed upon me that my brother would need it. He came to me later and told me that he had been in his room and seen a demon. He got out his Bible and read Psalm 91, and the evil spirit immediately fled.

I knew that **Psalm 91** would have this kind of impact because I had used it myself in the past when under severe attack. I often declare it prior to doing ministry events or when I know I am going into the enemy territory during intercession and evangelism. Satan is easily threatened and fearful himself of the people of God. He knows that if we know our identity and we are rooted in the Word of God, that he will not be able to defeat us.

So often, when God calls us to face giants, Satan will do his very best to create fear, intimidation, manipulation, and coercion to dissuade us. When David faced Goliath and the Philistine army Goliath mocked him and God.

> *"And the Philistine said to David, "Am I a dog, that you come to me with sticks?" And the Philistine cursed David by his gods. The Philistine said to David, "Come to me, and I will give your flesh to the birds of the air and to the beasts of the field."*
> **1 Samuel 17:43-44 ESV**

Remember, that Goliath himself likely lacked the understanding of the power of God. However, the principalities that motivated Goliath and the Philistines to oppose God's people know full well that David's God is the Most High God. They influence Goliaths threats.

Fear Tactics

- Mocking
- Insults
- Curses
- Threats

Thankfully, David knew the truth. He knew that His God, IS God! So, he responds to Goliath in this way...

> *"You come to me with a sword and with a spear and with a javelin, but I come to you in the name of the LORD of hosts, the God of the armies of Israel, whom you have defied."*
> **1 Samuel 17:45 ESV**

David successfully takes Goliath down with one stone and then cuts off the giant's head with the warriors own sword. The entire Philistine army flees. David had remembered the Word of God. He knew that God was "The Lord of Hosts." Throughout his life, David wrote many powerful Psalms to the Lord and the Lord delivered David from his enemies.

CALL TO ACTION

 ## PRAYING SCRIPTURE

When fear attempts to creep in and the accuser is at the door, use these scriptures that David used in times of trouble. Speak them out loud as you call upon the Lord. Let the demons hear your petitions and they will flee just as they did before. Allow it to penetrate your heart and mind as you cling to it like a sword and stand upon it like a rock. Satan knows that the Words of the Lord stand through the ages.

Psalm 91

ESV

"He who dwells in the shelter of the Most High will abide in the shadow of the Almighty. I will say to the LORD, "My refuge and my fortress, my God, in whom I trust." For he will deliver you from the snare of the fowler and from the deadly pestilence. He will cover you with his pinions, and under his wings you will find refuge; his faithfulness is a shield and buckler. You will not fear the terror of the night, nor the arrow that flies by day, nor the pestilence that stalks in darkness, nor the destruction that wastes at noonday. A thousand may fall at your side, ten thousand at your right hand, but it will not come near you. You will only look with your eyes and see the recompense of the wicked.

Because you have made the LORD your dwelling place – the Most High, who is my refuge – no evil shall be allowed to befall you, no plague come near your tent. For he will command his angels concerning you to guard you in all your ways. On their hands they will bear you up, lest you strike your foot against a stone. You will tread on the lion and the adder; the young lion and the serpent you will trample underfoot. "Because he holds fast to me in love, I will deliver him; I will protect him, because he knows my name. When he calls to me, I will answer him; I will be with him in trouble; I will rescue him and honor him. With long life I will satisfy him and show him my salvation."

Psalm 61:1-4

ESV

"Hear my cry, O God, listen to my prayer; from the end of the earth I call to you when my heart is faint. Lead me to the rock that is higher than I, for you have been my refuge, a strong tower against the enemy. Let me dwell in your tent forever! Let me take refuge under the shelter of your wings!"

Psalm 139:1-12

ESV

"You have searched me, LORD, and you know me. You know when I sit and when I rise; you perceive my thoughts from afar. You discern my going out and my lying down; you are familiar with all my ways. Before a word is on my tongue you, LORD, know it completely. You hem me in behind and before, and you lay your hand upon me. Such knowledge is too wonderful for me, too lofty for me to attain. Where can I go from your Spirit? Where can I flee from your presence? If I go up to the heavens, you are there; if I make my bed in the depths, you are there. If I rise on the wings of the dawn, if I settle on the far side of the sea, even there your hand will guide me, your right hand will hold me fast. If I say, "Surely the darkness will hide me and the light become night around me," even the darkness will not be dark to you; the

night will shine like the day, for darkness is as light to you."

Psalm 23

ESV

The LORD is my shepherd; I shall not want. He makes me lie down in green pastures. He leads me beside still waters. He restores my soul. He leads me in paths of righteousness for his name's sake. Even though I walk through the valley of the shadow of death, I will fear no evil, for you are with me; your rod and your staff, they comfort me. You prepare a table before me in the presence of my enemies; you anoint my head with oil; my cup overflows. Surely goodness and mercy shall follow me all the days of my life, and I shall dwell in the house of the LORD forever.

Psalm 27

ESV

"The LORD is my light and my salvation; whom shall I fear? The LORD is the stronghold of my life; of whom shall I be afraid? When evildoers assail me to eat up my flesh, my adversaries and foes, it is they who stumble and fall. Though an army encamp against me, my heart shall not fear; though war arise against me, yet I will be confident. One thing have I asked of the LORD, that will I seek after: that I may dwell in the house of the LORD all the days of my life, to gaze upon the beauty of the LORD and to inquire in his temple. For he will hide me in his shelter in the day of trouble; he will conceal me under the cover of his tent; he will lift me high upon a rock. And now my head shall be lifted up above my enemies all around me, and I will offer in his tent sacrifices with shouts of joy; I will sing and make melody to the LORD. Hear, O

LORD, when I cry aloud; be gracious to me and answer me! You have said, "Seek my face." My heart says to you, "Your face, LORD, do I seek." Hide not your face from me. Turn not your servant away in anger, O you who have been my help. Cast me not off; forsake me not, O God of my salvation! For my father and my mother have forsaken me, but the LORD will take me in. Teach me your way, O LORD, and lead me on a level path because of my enemies. Give me not up to the will of my adversaries; for false witnesses have risen against me, and they breathe out violence. I believe that I shall look upon the goodness of the LORD in the land of the living! Wait for the LORD; be strong, and let your heart take courage; wait for the Lord."

IN SUMMARY – PRAYING SCRIPTURE OUT LOUD

- Praying scripture out loud is a powerful weapon of warfare

- When we pray God's words out loud the enemy will flee

- Satan will try to dissuade you from believing these words and living them out

- Satan will commonly attempt to attack us with fear to dissuade us from doing the things God has called us to do

- David faced Goliath and Goliath attempted to scare him with mocking, insults, cursing, and threats

- David knew the Word of God and he was able to face Goliath and kill him with confidence. The entire Philistine army fled

- Raise your sword – the Word of God – and petition the Lord. The Lord delivered David and He will deliver you

Concluding Prayer

"Your word is a lamp to my feet and a light to my path."
Psalm 119:105 ESV

Lord Jesus, you are the Alpha and the Omega, the Beginning, and the End. Nothing is too big for you, my God, my Rock, my Refuge in times of trouble. Father, I surrender all my fears, my *"what if"* questions, my unknowns, that which is out of my control, my anxious thoughts, my imagination, and my desire to try to fix everything on my own. Freely, I give them to you, Lord. I lay them at your feet.

Instead of fear, I choose peace. Instead of worry, I choose joy. Instead of sleeplessness, I choose rest. Your name is higher than any other name, and your ways are higher than my ways. My Good Shepherd, I know you lead me in and out and to find pasture. I will dwell in your house and walk in the covering of your wings. Even when chaos surrounds me, I will have peace in my mind and my heart. I choose the peace that surpasses understanding that you have promised. I receive this peace now in Jesus' name.

Concluding Prayer

There is no other name in Heaven or on Earth by which I can be saved. You have called me by name, and I have cried out to you with my unyielding, "YES!" I am yours, and you are mine. I will walk in courage and strength and fearlessness all the days of my life. Wherever I go, fear will flee, and peace will enter every place that I step foot. Your perfect love has cast out all my fears. Who the Son sets free is truly free. I am free. I am free. I am free indeed.

Glory be to God in the Highest Heaven. May your name be magnified with my life. Hosanna blessed is the one who has come in the name of the Lord. Hallelujah. In Jesus' name I pray, Amen and

Review and Activation

Answer Key on Page 76

Across

[3] This is where the enemy focuses his attacks on us. He knows that if he can influence this effectively he will be able to impact our lives significantly.

[5] Jesus promises to give this to us in all circumstances. It is a gift that surpasses all human understanding and we are to share it with others.

[10] This part of the armor of God guards our heart. The Holy Spirit is continually guiding us in this and helping us to obey and honor the Lord.

[12] This holds up the rest of the armor and it is the foundation of our freedom in Christ. Jesus says if we know this, it will set us free.

[13] This is one of the names of Jesus because we are like his sheep. He leads us beside quiet waters and green pastures and he protects is in dark valleys.

Down

[1] A Shield to extinguish the fiery arrows of the enemy. This is what we must have instead of doubt.

[2] This part of us is our mind, heart, and emotions.

[4] This guards the mind like a helmet. We have been given this as a gift and because of it our name is written in the Book of Life.

[6] This is a birthright as children of God. We are to use this to trample on snakes and scorpions and Jesus promises that nothing will harm us.

[7] This is breathed out by God and it is good for teaching, rebuking and training.

[8] This is a vocal remission of something or someone. We should do this to break agreements with lies and with assignments of the enemy.

[9] We must do this in all circumstances because our own understanding is not what we base our faith on. If we do this we can rest even when we do not know what lay ahead

[11] A weapon that represents the Word of God.

Activation

List some thoughts you have had that do not align with the Word of God and commit to stop partnering with them.

"I no longer partner with the thought that…"

1._____
2._____
3._____

List three truths from the Word of God that you choose to partner with instead of the thoughts listed above.

"I choose to partner with the truth, which is…"

1._____
2._____
3._____

Choose three key scriptures that build up your faith and commit to memorize them.

1._____
2._____
3._____

Review and Activation

Write down some prayers that the Lord has answered for you.

_____

_____

_____

Write down some things that you are still praying for and commit to trust the Lord with them.

_____

_____

_____

Write down at least three words to describe what the Lord says about you and your identity in Christ.

_____

_____

_____

Review and Activation

Answer Key

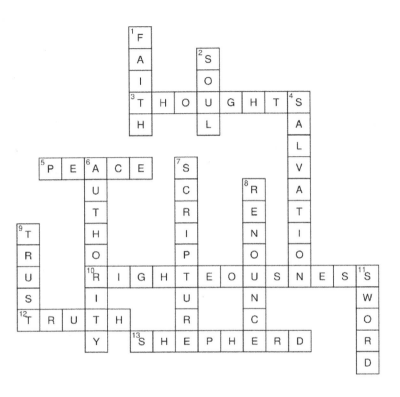

A Note from the Author

Thank you for reading my book! I pray that it will be a tool in your hand for overcoming fear and walking in the peace of the Lord. Standing in peace is a daily journey and as we invite the Lord into our process, He is so good to show us how to combat the lies that the enemy throws at us.

If you enjoyed this book, you may also enjoy free teaching blogs, videos, and other resources that can be found on my website : www.wesleyrejoiced.com.

Your feedback is welcome, and you can send me your thoughts and questions here: info@wesleyrejoiced.com

Blessings upon Blessings,

Wesley Lewis

ISBN: 978-0-578-98976-1

Made in the USA
Las Vegas, NV
04 November 2021